Becoming Barnabas:

A Ministry of Coming Alongside

By Robert E. Logan and Tara Miller

Published by ChurchSmart Resources

We are an evangelical Christian publisher committed to producing excellent products at affordable prices to help church leaders accomplish effective ministry in the areas of church planting, church growth, church renewal and leadership development.

For a free catalog of our resources call 1-800-253-4276.
Visit us at www.ChurchSmart.com

Cover design by: Robert Rummel
Edited by: Phil Newell

ISBN: 978-1-936812-09-7

Contents

Chapter 1: Who was Barnabas? 5
How to be a world changer without anybody even knowing your name

Chapter 2: What does it look like to be a Barnabas?.....................11
The quiet power of listening and asking good questions

Chapter 3: Why do we need more Barnabases? 19
What a difference it makes in your ministry

Chapter 4: A Barnabas future 25
Imagine what the world could look like

Chapter 5: How can you develop a Barnabas culture? 33
Practical steps and options

Chapter 1

Who was Barnabas?

How to be a world changer without anybody even knowing your name

Once upon a time there was a young guy on a ministry team. He was new to leadership, pretty inexperienced, and did a stupid thing. His mistake was a setback to the whole ministry and he didn't handle the situation well. The team leader was angry with him and kicked him off the team.

Then another member of the ministry team, one with experience and patience, stepped in and said, "Wait, let me work with him. I believe he can learn from his mistakes and still make a contribution to this ministry."

Sound familiar? You may have even had some names come to mind as you read this story. Situations like this happen all the time in ministry. But the story I'm thinking of took place over 2,000 years ago. The young leader was John Mark. The team leader was the Apostle Paul. And the team member who stepped in was Barnabas.

This book is about the Barnabases in our world: the people who are instrumental in developing others, the people we haven't heard of, the people who are rarely in the spotlight themselves but make that spotlight a reality for others.

Are you called to be a Barnabas? Barnabases are people who empower others through encouragement, support, and prayer. They develop and bring out the leadership gifts in others and ensure that no one is working in isolation. They create an environment that brings out the best in people and empowers them to do all they can for the Kingdom of God.

If God is calling you to serve as a Barnabas, you have an essential role to play. Barnabases make a deep and significant difference in our world. Let's start by taking a look at the original Barnabas.

Barnabas: the son of encouragement

I consider Barnabas to be one of the most important people in the Bible, yet he gets almost no recognition. He probably wouldn't even make most people's biblical top ten list. In fact, most people don't even know his real name: Joseph. Barnabas was a nickname given to him by the apostles; it means "son of encouragement" (Acts 4:34-37). The word encouragement literally means "the one called alongside to help." His story is told throughout the book of Acts.

We first meet Barnabas after he sold a field and brought the money to the apostles. He became fully integrated into the early church, preached the gospel, brought people to the Lord, and earned a good reputation. Acts 11:24 says that "Barnabas was a good man, full of the Holy Spirit and strong in faith."

It was Barnabas who sponsored Paul in among the other Apostles. Paul, then called Saul, was cut off from the church and widely feared as an infamous persecutor of Christians. When he claimed conversion, most believers thought it was a trap. Barnabas went to find Paul and brought him to the Apostles. It was only because Barnabas vouched for Paul that the other apostles were willing to meet with him.

As the Apostle Paul increasingly began exercising his leadership gifts, Barnabas traveled with him and worked effectively alongside him, bringing encouragement and strength. As they worked together, they began to be referred to as "Paul and Barnabas," rather than "Barnabas and Paul." When that shift happened, there were none of the ego wars we might expect. In fact, I suspect that Barnabas considered his ministry successful precisely because of this shift. He had successfully supported and empowered the Apostle Paul.

Just as Barnabas helped bring Paul into the good graces of the other apostles, he functioned in a similar restorative capacity with John Mark. John Mark, brought along as an assistant on some travels, had the unhappy history of bailing on a missionary journey, leaving the mission in jeopardy. As a consequence, Paul refused to work with him and he was sidelined from future ministry.

Barnabas disagreed sharply with Paul, and they parted ways: Paul with Silas and Barnabas with John Mark. Only Barnabas believed in John Mark's potential for future meaningful work. When everyone else considered him unfit for ministry, Barnabas journeyed with him and worked toward his restoration. That restoration did come about, and we see in Paul's later writings how important John Mark eventually became to him in his ministry.

Barnabas had that rare and powerful quality of believing in people and seeing their potential even when others would not. Barnabas was someone who, instead of taking center stage himself, empowered others.

Consider the long-term significance of the role Barnabas played in supporting Paul and John Mark. If we take them out the equation, how much of the New Testament wouldn't even be written? Remember that Paul led Luke to Christ, so we're talking about the gospel of Mark, the gospel of Luke, the book of Acts, and all of Paul's letters. How much of the near east would never have heard the gospel? Now that's a contribution to the Kingdom.

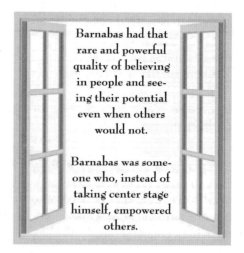

Barnabas had that rare and powerful quality of believing in people and seeing their potential even when others would not.

Barnabas was someone who, instead of taking center stage himself, empowered others.

What Barnabas can do

Imagine what a difference you could make as a Barnabas. Who could you help and encourage? How could you provide support for them? What kind of impact might that have for the Kingdom?

Now imagine a whole host of people in your church equipped to encourage and spur one another on toward more fruitful ministry. What kind of multiplying effect would that have? How many leaders wouldn't burn out? How many struggling parents or spouses could be helped? How many new teachers and group leaders could be developed and supported? How many new ministries to the community could be launched?

Almost all churches want to develop disciples and ministry leaders. They want a system of relational support that nurtures and supports their leaders. They want to empower people in their congregations to make full use of the gifts entrusted to them by the Holy Spirit. They want a structure of leader-care that is flexible enough and relational enough to grow along with the growth of the church.

All of this can be accomplished through intentional Barnabas relationships. Becoming Barnabas can help people...

- experience God
- respond to the Spirit
- engage authentically in relationships
- serve sacrificially
- be transformed personally
- live generously
- become disciplemakers
- impact the broader community

If more people were living like this, just imagine what could be accomplished for the Kingdom.

Barnabas and coaching

We use coaching and Barnabas ministry interchangeably in this book. Coaching is a fine term, and if it works in your context, use it. However, sometimes it has the wrong connotations.

When I was in Japan many years ago, I was describing coaching. The translator who was working with me told me point blank that the word "coach" would not work in the Japanese context. "A coach is someone who yells at you, who humiliates and shames you – even at times physically beating you," he explained. "I don't think that's what you're getting at here."

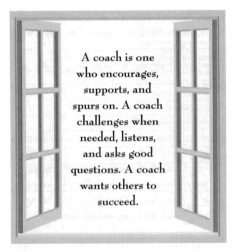

A coach is one who encourages, supports, and spurs on. A coach challenges when needed, listens, and asks good questions. A coach wants others to succeed.

Indeed not. A coach is one who encourages, supports, and spurs on. A coach challenges when needed, listens, and asks good questions. A coach wants others to succeed and connects them with the resources they need to do so.

In the United States, likely no one has an issue with the word coach like the one that surfaced in Japan. However, with the rise of life coaching, executive coaching, and career coaching, the term can carry a connotation of highly trained professionalism… something out of reach for the average person in the church who just wants to help out and already has a day job.

If that's the case in your church, just call it Barnabas ministry as they do in Japan. After all, the original Barnabas didn't engage in any professional-level training in order to do his ministry. He simply made the most of the gifts God gave him to support and encourage others in their ministries. You – and others in your church – can certainly do the same. It's not out of reach.

Consider the ways coaches make a difference in sports, drawing out and developing the God-given talents of the players. Michael Jordan is arguably the best basketball player who has ever played the game. All over the world people have heard of him. In rural China, "Jordan rules" can be seen written on basketball backboards. Michael Jordan was a star, the best player on his team – on any team. He could shoot three-pointers and do long slam dunks. Athletic shoes were named after him. He was a leader admired across the world.

For the first six years of his professional career, Michael Jordan won scoring titles, defensive player of the year, and many other awards. Yet during those same six years, he never won any championships. Michael was a star, but not a champion.

At that point, Phil Jackson became the coach for the Chicago Bulls. Phil taught a system called the triangle offense, which requires trusting your team. Now Phil had played pro ball, but he didn't have the innate skill Jordan had. But Phil had a way with the team, and he had a framework that allowed the team to work together within a structure: the triangle offense. People called Phil the Zen master. He was known for bringing non-traditional methods into his coaching, and he aimed for a holistic experience with his players. He said to Michael, "You're going to have to trust in me, and you're going to have to trust in your team. You've been trying to do it on your own up until now." Jordan bought in. He started passing the ball and playing as a member of the team.

The team began winning and didn't stop. They won six championships in the early 90's. They became a dynasty. Once they started functioning as a team, once Michael Jordan put his trust in a coach, the Bulls were able to make history. They accomplished all they wanted and more. Jordan was a hero, and the Bulls went on to win six championships.

It doesn't matter how gifted someone is – how strong their God-given talent is, how good their skills are – no one can do it all alone. Coaches make a difference not only in sports, but in ministry. We can come alongside people and empower them to live out their calling to the best of their ability. To do so, they need coaches and teammates.

Sometimes one simple question can make all the difference. I once was talking with a man who was overseeing a training process to prepare people for ministry. I asked him, "When people finish your process, what can they do?"

That question, he told me later, kept him up at night. It eventually prompted him to shift from having those he was training master information to having them actually live out ministry skills. It made a difference, resulting in the kind of discipleship that shapes the character while living out the values of the Kingdom.

In another case, I was working with a man who needed help tackling blockages in his life that were holding him back – time management, money management, that kind of thing. Through our dialogue, he discovered his God-given gifts and passion, and was led into a powerful ministry of leading worship. The man went from just having a job to fulfilling his calling in significant ways. Over time his ministry has expanded to helping others live lives of holistic worship.

Listening well to people and asking them good questions really matters. Being a Barnabas really matters.

The rest of this book lays out the core skills you need to live as a Barnabas within the Kingdom of God. If you serve faithfully and well in this way, you may never be in the spotlight and people may not even know your name, but think of the difference you will have made in the lives of individuals and on the church as a whole.

Reflection questions:

1. What insights do you draw from the story of Barnabas?
2. Who has served as a Barnabas in your life?
3. How are you called to be a Barnabas to others?
4. What do you think God might do with several people serving as Barnabases within your community?

Chapter 2

What does it look like to be a Barnabas?

The quiet power of listening and asking good questions

A few years ago I was serving a team of ministry leaders working among the urban poor in Mexico City. They were doing hard work – the kind of work that can leave you discouraged and feeling like you're not making much of a difference. My job was to encourage them. As I looked out at their faces, tired but hopeful, I gave them an assignment.

I introduced these six questions, originally used by Carl George. I like to call them *The Barnabas Questions*:

- How are you?
- What are you celebrating?
- What challenges are you experiencing?
- What do you plan to do about these challenges?
- How can I help you?
- How can I pray for you?

I instructed the group to break into pairs and spend the next half hour walking through these questions together. The members of this team had been working closely together for a long time, and felt they already knew one another well.

Yet as they asked each other questions like, "What are you celebrating?" and really listened to the answers, taking time to draw each other out, something shifted. The team members began

Having someone really listen to you is like taking a sip of water and realizing how thirsty you are.

experiencing a whole new level of intentionality, support, and encouragement. It's like taking a sip of water and realizing how thirsty you were.

Then I told them the biblical story of Barnabas. "If you do your job well as a Barnabas, few people will even know about you. Others will get the credit, but you'll have really made a difference by empowering them."

Some of them had tears in their eyes as they considered their potential impact. Yet I could see the doubt too: "Who am I that I can make a difference?" I could see them wondering: "I'm just an ordinary follower of Jesus who sometimes stumbles and falls, who doesn't always know what to say. Could I really function as a Barnabas?"

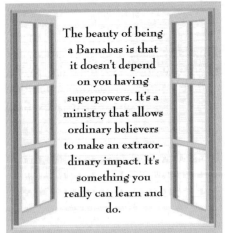

The beauty of being a Barnabas is that it doesn't depend on you having superpowers. It's a ministry that allows ordinary believers to make an extraordinary impact. It's something you really can learn and do.

Those team members now use the Barnabas questions with those they serve and partner alongside in the community. Who knows what leaders they will raise up from the slums of Mexico City? Apostles have come from stranger places.

The beauty of being a Barnabas is that it doesn't depend on you having superpowers. It's a ministry that allows ordinary believers to make an extraordinary impact.

I've found there's a scarcity of real listening in our world. We listen for information when we feel the need for it. We listen in sound bites. We listen so we will know what we can say in response. We listen to bolster our own perspective or further our own agenda.

Most people – especially ministry leaders – don't have someone who regularly takes the time to truly listen to them with focused attention. I've seen it time and time again as I've taught coach training events. When I assign people 30 minutes of uninterrupted, focused time when someone else is really listening to them, asking questions, and encouraging them to share more, they're amazed at the simple power of that experience. They recognize it as the rare gift that it is.

As a Barnabas, you can give that gift to others. The rest of this chapter walks you through the two most important skills of a Barnabas: listening well and asking good questions. These two skills alone will get you 90% of the way there. And they're something anyone can do with practice.

Discovery listening

Discovery listening means listening in order to discover the other person, listening out of curiosity, listening without your own agenda. It's based on the principle that people learn better when they discover for themselves. When we practice this skill, we move from being the expert-with-the-answers to being someone who helps others discover their own answers. With that foundation, people are able to move forward more effectively.

I tried an experiment one time. Every time someone came to me with a question, a problem, or a request for advice, I did not immediately provide an answer. Before I gave my input, I would first fully unpack their best thinking. See the conversation below as an example:

- **Youth pastor:** "Bob, I've got some new kids from the community who have started attending some youth group events – which is great – but I've never met their parents. I'm not sure how to engage the parents or reach out to them. Any advice?"
- **Bob:** "I'm happy to give you some advice. But the way you've asked the question tells me you've already given quite a bit of thought to this issue. What has already become clear to you?"
- **Youth pastor:** "I could ask the kids for their parents' phone numbers and just call them, but that feels a little strange – kind of like cold-calling." (Pauses and looks at me, waiting.)
- **Bob:** "So one approach is to just call the parents. But that feels a bit awkward. What else have you thought of?"
- **Youth pastor:** "Well, I've been wondering about doing a family event to try to bring in some of the parents and siblings, but I'm not sure what kind of event would work well." (Pause.)
- **Bob:** "So doing a family event might be a possibility. Tell me about that."
- **Youth pastor:** "I could do a family movie and pizza night with an open gym. That way kids would invite their own parents."
- **Bob:** "Hmm… tell me more."
- **Youth pastor:** "Seems like it'd be a safe and comfortable place for people to talk and hang out in a non-threatening way. Some of the youth leaders might begin to develop relationships with the parents and the parents might start to feel more comfortable with the church… (et cetera, et cetera, et cetera). Thanks for your input, Bob. That was really helpful."

You'll notice I didn't actually give him any input. By the time we got to that point, he didn't need it anymore. But I appreciated the thanks anyway!

Discovery listening means letting someone think out loud and listening in on their conversation, just repeating back what you are hearing without putting any spin on it.

I've had different versions of this conversation over and over again. When people would approach me, I'd listen to their question, then ask, "What do you think?" I would listen, then summarize without evaluating or interpreting. I'd invite them to say more: "What else?" I'd refrain from giving any input until I'd exhausted their thinking.

Only when they couldn't think of anything else to say did I give input... if it was still needed. Usually it wasn't. During the course of my experiment, I found that about 70% of the time people would come up with their own perfectly fine answer without any input from me. Listening alone was helpful to them.

Discovery listening means letting someone think out loud and repeating back what you are hearing without putting any spin on it.

Here's how you can practice discovery listening:
1. Focus: Give your undivided attention
2. Summarize: Mirror back what you hear the other person saying
3. Unpack: Invite them to expand their thinking by asking "What else?" or "Tell me more?"

Try practicing discovery listening for 30 days. When you are intentional about the way you listen and practice the steps above, you'll be surprised by the impact it has on the people around you. You'll likely also realize how rare real listening actually is.

Asking good questions

To listening, we add a second skill: asking good questions. A Barnabas is someone who asks good questions, and sometimes that makes all the difference.

I was listening to someone recently who was upset about a particular situation. He'd been venting for a while, when I asked, "What do you want?" "What I want is for [coworker] to work with me, not against me," he blurted. Then he stopped, and there was dead silence. He'd had a profound realization. He realized that his answer cut to the very core of the issue. The simple clarity of that realization gave him the insight to know how to move forward. Sometimes a simple question can bring about a significant breakthrough.

Let's take another example. A young man had recently broken up with a girl in the church. In the midst of all the injustice and hurt he felt, what he wanted was to write a Facebook post blasting his ex-girlfriend. The person he was talking with, who was serving as a Barnabas, asked, "What would you like this relationship to be like in one year?" It was a question crafted to provide long-term perspective.

The young man articulated what he wanted the relationship to look like a year from now – a vision that included civil connections. The next question his friend asked: "How does that long-term goal affect what you're planning to write?" The slanderous Facebook post didn't happen, because good questions helped the young man gain perspective and clarity on how to move forward productively.

Notice something about these three questions:
- What do you want?
- What would you like this relationship to be like in one year?
- How does that long-term goal affect what you're planning to write?

All of them are what we call open-ended questions. They cannot be answered by yes or no. They require thought and input from the person on the receiving end of the question. Closed questions, on the other hand, collapse the vision. They don't require as much investment from the person being asked the question, but rather keep the asker in control.

Look at some of the very simple examples below:

Closed questions	Open questions
Would you like to order pizza for lunch?	What would you like to do for lunch?
Have you considered a PowerPoint presentation?	How would you like to present the material to the team?

Often closed questions are not really questions at all – just veiled suggestions. They don't promote creativity or free thinking. Potential responses or categories are already in the mind of the questioner.

The challenge in learning how to ask open-ended questions is that from an early age our parents exposed us to closed questions:
- Did you remember to____?
- Do you want X or Y?
- Did you do your chores?

In school we are given true-false and multiple-choice questions, so we learn to gather information through closed questions.

Good questions move conversations deeper. They draw others out. Have you ever walked away from a conversation and thought, "Wow, that person was so easy to talk to – what a great conversation!" Odds are you just talked with someone who knows how to ask good questions.

Examples of good questions:

- What are your options?
- What's really important?
- What else needs to be done?
- What obstacles are you facing?
- What do you want to accomplish?
- What are possible ways to get there?
- Which path will you choose?

When we ask questions well, we can help people reflect, increase their awareness, and take responsibility for the direction they're going. We also tacitly recognize the power of the Holy Spirit to speak to others and to guide them. If he is leading them, we don't have to. We are free to listen.

Here are some tips for listening well and asking good questions:

- Take the time necessary to listen – don't be in a hurry.
- When you're listening, focus on the other person not on what you're going to say next.
- Summarize what you're hearing the person say.
- Invite the person to say more.
- Ask open-ended questions to draw out a person's thoughts.
- If someone pauses after you ask a question or they say, "That's a good question," don't say anything. Just wait in silence and give them time to think.

Exercise: This week when you talk with a family member, friend, or co-worker, see how long you can listen and ask questions before you start interjecting your thoughts or making statements.

The test of a Barnabas

Listening well and asking good questions are the two hallmarks of a Barnabas. These are qualities we see in the original Barnabas. When he was sent from Jerusalem to Antioch, he looked around, saw the work that God was already doing, and encouraged the people in that work.

> When the church at Jerusalem heard what had happened, they sent Barnabas to Antioch. When he arrived and saw this evidence of God's blessing, he was filled with joy, and he encouraged the believers to stay true to the Lord. Barnabas was a good man, full of the Holy Spirit and strong in faith. And many people were brought to the Lord. (Acts 11:22-24)

It wasn't about Barnabas himself, or what a great difference he could make in the ministry. It was about seeing, affirming, and cooperating with how the Holy Spirit was already at work.

Likewise, if you serve as a Barnabas, it won't be about you. It will be about those you are serving. You're not lording it over others, but coming alongside others, helping them move toward where they sense God leading them.

So often we think we need to have the answers. But that's not the call of a Barnabas. A Barnabas is called to be helpful, not the expert. As people talk with you, they can sense whether or not you are a Barnabas. They are asking three questions: Can I trust you? Are you helpful? Do you care? If they determine that all three questions can be answered yes, they will look to you as a Barnabas.

Reflection questions:

1. Think of a time you were asked a really good question. What was the impact?
2. When have you felt you were listening well?
3. In what contexts can you practice discovery listening and asking good questions?
4. What blockages do you face to listening well? To asking good questions?
5. What can you start doing differently now?

Chapter 3

Why do we need more Barnabases?

What a difference it makes in your ministry

I heard two men talking in a public restroom: "I saw a great movie this weekend," said one. "Me too," replied the other. Then they left.
— Larry Crabb

How many of the conversations in your church sound like that one? It's so easy for people to exchange information, telling others about themselves and their own experiences without engaging with the other person much at all.

Those conversations don't always look odd on the surface, but when you bring people together who do not listen to each other well and who do not ask questions well, the resulting relationships can be challenging.

This chapter takes a closer look at what a church or ministry looks like when there are a lot of Barnabases – and what it looks like when there aren't. The presence or absence of Barnabases can make all the difference between good small groups and bad small groups, good dinner gatherings and bad dinner gatherings, good parenting ministries and bad parenting ministries.

My wife and I recently had another couple over for dinner. About half an hour into our time together I realized I was feeling a bit depleted, as if I was working hard. Then I realized that the other couple hadn't asked us a single question.

I started paying closer attention. Janet and I were asking questions, listening, asking follow-up questions. We were learning a lot about this other couple, their interests, their children, what their day-to-day life was like. But no questions were being asked in return. A couple of times Janet volunteered a bit of information about us. The other couple seemed to hear it, but didn't pick up on it or ask any follow-up questions. It felt like a really long evening.

They seemed like a nice, well-meaning couple who wanted to engage but didn't quite know how. I wondered how different our dinner conversation might have been if they had received a bit of instruction and practice in how to be a Barnabas.

Contrast that evening with another dinner at my house. Couple number two asked us how we met, how we came to be a part of our current church, what we thought about various local issues. They were curious about us and seemed to genuinely want to get to know us. Sometimes it was even hard to find an opening to ask questions back so we could hear from them! By the end of the evening, there was much laughter and conversation and I found myself feeling energized rather than drained.

Is it just that couple number two were better people than couple number one? Not at all. Although skills such as listening, asking good questions, and focusing on other people come more naturally to some people than others, anyone can learn them. Often people simply don't know what a dramatic difference these skills make in their social interactions. With practice, anyone can begin to live into these behaviors more naturally.

The difference a Barnabas can make in a church

So how does being a Barnabas make a difference in our churches, groups, and ministries? What kinds of interactions result? Let's take a look at one very simple example, and draw some conclusions from it.

Several families had just gathered together for their weekly community group meeting. They were standing around the kitchen, snacking on some cheese and crackers. One ten-year-old complained that his school had just decided to make the switch to uniforms for all the kids: "Uniforms don't let you express your individuality!"

A woman standing nearby (not his mom) nodded in understanding and asked, "What are some other ways you could express your individuality?" The boy seized on the question and ran with it, coming up with at least three good ways to express his individuality within in a few minutes.

What observations can you make from this story? (If this were a teaching environment, I would wait for your observations, but as it's a book I'll need to go ahead and just give you mine. Alas, the limitations of print.)

- The woman acknowledged the boy's frustration and didn't try to explain why uniforms would be good. Trying to convince the boy to change his mind about uniforms would have been many people's first response, and he would almost certainly have dug in his heels and argued further.

- She asked for his thoughts in a way that shifted his focus from what he could not do toward what he could do. That's huge.

- The boy was asked for his thoughts and listened to by an adult who was not his parent. That's rare, and opens up dialogue across generational lines.

- The boy left the conversation feeling empowered, like he had options. That's the opposite of how he felt coming into the conversation.

We need more Barnabases in our groups, in our churches, in our ministries, in our neighborhoods – everywhere! Imagine community groups filled with people asking questions, displaying curiosity and other-centeredness. Imagine people really listening instead of trying to change your mind or just waiting for their turn to talk. If one Barnabas can make a big difference, imagine what a whole host of Barnabases spread throughout your ministry could do!

Here are some common issues Barnabases could help resolve:

- Lay leader burnout and turnover: "Do I have to do this ministry forever?"
- Lack of oversight and support of small groups: "No one in the leadership even knows what's going on in my small group!"
- People not fitting well in their service roles: "I'm doing this to serve the church, not because it's my calling."
- Leaders stagnating rather than growing in their skills: "I've been doing this forever and I know how."
- Pastoral burnout. See Jethro's advice to Moses: *"What you are doing is not good. You and these people who come to you will only wear yourselves out. The work is too heavy for you; you cannot handle it alone."* (Exodus 18:17-18)
- Lack of infrastructure to support growth: "Right now we're a small church, healthy and growing, with six community groups. It works for now, but it won't work in a couple more years."

A Barnabas for each ministry?

Consider what a difference a Barnabas or two in each of your ministries might make. Think of any of the various ministries your church might have: the youth group, the marriage ministry, the parenting workshops, the homeless outreach, the Sunday school classes, the missional community engagement, the worship team.

Imagine these scenarios:

- A Barnabas helping a leader take the time to process what he really wants in life and in ministry
- A Barnabas helping someone find a ministry role that's more in line with her calling and gifts
- A Barnabas helping a new believer process how best to reach out to his neighbors
- A Barnabas helping a ministry leader feel supported and empowered rather than just told what to do
- A Barnabas helping a believer take the next steps in her discipleship

Wouldn't all of that be an amazing expression of the Kingdom of God?

Fill in the blank with a ministry you have and consider how God might use a Barnabas in that context:

Consider every church leader's favorite event: the board meeting. Instead of everyone just spouting opinions and waiting for their turn for rebuttal, what if people started asking great questions? The power of a decision is in direct proportion to the quality of the questions that were asked while making it. If you ask lousy questions, you come up with simplistic, shortsighted answers.

Bonus: Some good all-purpose questions for board meetings
- What principles do we need to consider as we approach this decision?
- What are the criteria we want to use to evaluate a possible course of action?
- What are we trying to accomplish? How will we know if we did?

- What do people have to lose? What do they have to gain?
- How will we help people embrace the change?
- When and how will we communicate this decision?

Let's take a sample meeting where board members are analyzing how to encourage people toward greater financial giving. In addition to the questions above, someone asks, "What are the blockages people face related to financial giving?"

This question gives rise to all sorts of thoughts and observations that help the board get to the roots of the issue. Some people have the heart to give but don't know how to manage their money. Other people have wrongly bought into the value of accumulating more. Some simply don't understand the reasons for giving, either biblically or practically. Yet others think there isn't enough transparency about what is done with money that is given.

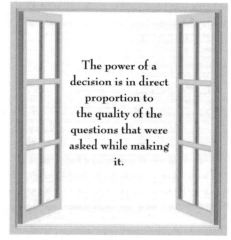

The power of a decision is in direct proportion to the quality of the questions that were asked while making it.

When the board examines the blockages, they open up all kinds of possible ways to address them. Generally speaking, if you reduce the negative forces, you move the ball forward. That's a lot more effective – and more biblical – than simply pushing people to give more.

Think about what a difference good questions could make on your ministry teams. Say the outreach team is sitting down to evaluate the effectiveness of the food pantry ministry. What would happen if they asked these questions?

- What's working?
- What's not working?
- What are we learning?
- What needs to change?
- What's next?

The team could suddenly recognize that although they are distributing food to the poor, they are not building relationships as much as they could. They are learning about the importance of relationship in service and giving. They could start discussing ways to make the food pantry more relational, and make plans to move in that direction.

What if there were Barnabases sprinkled throughout your church? You'd be getting the kind of real-world results you want to get. Barnabas behaviors make a difference in practical ways, from board meetings to dinner parties, from food pantries to interactions with kids.

A Barnabas-full environment looks dramatically different from a Barnabas-empty environment... and it will feel different to everyone who walks through your doors. They may not be able to put their finger on why it's different, but they will feel it.

Reflection questions:
1. Envision Barnabases throughout your church. Where might you place them? What might they do?
2. How would social interactions look different with the presence of more Barnabases?
3. What are some ways you could begin developing more Barnabases in your church? How could you introduce the concepts?
4. Make a list of all of the different ministries in your church. Consider the potential role of a Barnabas in each.

Ministry	Barnabas role

Chapter 4

A Barnabas future

Imagine what the world could look like

Barnabas ministry is simple, not complicated. It takes ordinary people wherever they're at and helps them move forward. It applies equally well to neighbors, new believers, leaders, parents, pastors, and people struggling with their jobs. Why? Because anyone who slows down enough to listen can hear the voice of the Holy Spirit. He is already at work.

In this chapter, let's take a tour together as silent observers of Barnabas behavior across a church and beyond.

• • • • •

Dana is a Barnabas currently serving as a missional community leader. She senses the need to take her group deeper into their discipleship journey, and so the group begins working through a resource Dana found called the *Dimensions of Discipleship* materials.

Since each person is in a different place in life with different needs, Dana breaks the group into triads so people can serve as Barnabases to one another. As each individual thinks through what they are hearing from God, they have two others who are listening to them, praying for them, and asking them questions.

• • • • •

Chad is part of one of these triads. He's been focusing on personal transformation. He's been struggling at his job, and feels that his current role as an engineer is limiting. At the same time, he's not sure what to do next and is afraid of making a big career change and then regretting it.

As Chad listens for the voice of the Holy Spirit, he senses that God may be calling him to teach inner city teens as the next step in his discipleship. But he's not sure. How could he know when he hasn't tried it? Through the other people in his triad asking open-ended questions, he remembers that his company has a leave of absence policy. He can take six months off and still come back to his engineering job afterwards if he wants to. That's just enough time to teach a semester of math at a struggling local middle school that is desperate for qualified math teachers.

Chad feels a sense of hope and expectation – along with a little trepidation – as he puts in for a leave of absence and begins a dialogue with the school principal.

· · · · ·

As Chad begins teaching, he gets to know Joaquin, a 7th grader who starts showing up at the voluntary "homework club" Chad has established after school. Joaquin seems to be having some trouble at home, and Chad starts asking questions. Apparently Joaquin's older brother is involved with some kids who are causing trouble around the neighborhood and they've been hanging around the family's house a lot, where there are three younger siblings.

Through a conference between Chad, Joaquin, and his mother (during which Chad serves as a Barnabas), the family decides to establish some boundaries to keep the older neighborhood teens out of their house and help Joaquin's brother make better choices.

· · · · ·

Joaquin's mother, Maria, sees the difference in her family after implementing some of the "advice" Chad gave her. She has forgotten that it was her idea and that Chad only listened and asked questions. Although Maria was raised Catholic, she has been far from the church for all of her adult life. She won't go so far as showing up at Chad's church (Would she fit in there? Probably not, she thinks.)

However, she does decide to show up at the women's Bible study on Tuesday morning. Just once, she tells herself. After all, there's free childcare. What can it hurt? Maria is surprised to find that the women there don't seem to be judgmental about her being a single mom. Some of the women are actually really nice to her and seem interested in her life. They ask questions and listen. They share honestly about their own lives and struggles.

Tuesday mornings quickly become one of the most restful and energizing times in Maria's otherwise very busy week. She's not entirely sure about Jesus or church yet, but these women seem all right.

. . . . .

Jennifer and Cynthia are two of the women in Maria's Tuesday morning Bible study. They both have young kids and are in the thick of all of the difficulties of that season of life: potty training, teaching toddlers to share, being woken up in the middle of the night, helping kindergarteners learn basic social skills. But they want more than to just survive this stage of life. As they've been talking with each other, praying, and listening for the voice of God in the midst of the chaos of life, they sense a desire to create a support network to help parents – and their children – thrive.

They create a network of parents who serve as Barnabases to other parents. They don't have to know everything about parenting. In fact, they are told not to try to impose their own views on other parents, but to listen and ask questions. Their goal is for the parents to have someone to listen to them and serve as a sounding board as they seek to become better parents.

. . . . .

As the parent network ministry takes off, Jason, the children's pastor, feels a dip in his job demands. Usually he feels overwhelmed by the needs, the scheduling, the complaints, the lack of volunteers, etc. But things have gotten better lately. Maybe it's due to that new parent network ministry… who knows? But whatever the reason, Jason is now able to take some time to sift through what he's hearing from God lately.

The truth is, Jason has not only been feeling overwhelmed, but also angry. He's had an ongoing conflict with the worship pastor for about six months and it has gotten close the boiling point. They are having difficulty working together and the resulting interpersonal conflict is interfering with both of their jobs. Jason is a bit afraid of taking the issue to Sam, the lead pastor, but he figures he's going to have to at some point, so he might as well get it over with.

Sam listens to Jason's perspective and empathizes without saying anything negative about Pete, the worship pastor. Jason is surprised how much better he feels after talking with Sam. So much better, in fact, that he agrees when Sam offers to help facilitate a conversation between Jason and Pete to try to help both of them feel better about their working environment and relationship.

• • • • •

Pete is surprised to have the conversation with Jason and Sam. He wasn't aware there was anything wrong, but then his mind has been on other things lately. Maybe he hasn't been paying as much attention as he should to the way he's impacting those around him.

Sam, the lead pastor, handles the situation with such grace that Pete decides to confide in him how stuck he's been feeling in his ministry. He feels like there's something next, something nagging at him that he needs to do, but it's just out of range.

Sam encourages him to think outside the box of "worship pastor." Maybe God is calling Pete to do something beyond that role. Over the next couple of months, Pete slowly puts together the pieces of a discipleship weekend. He doesn't want worship to be limited to Sunday mornings or devotional times. He wants to encourage people in the church to participate in whole-life worship: worshiping with their whole heart, soul, mind, and strength.

• • • • •

The weekend comes together, and fifteen people set aside time to reflect on their discipleship journeys. Three Barnabases are present to help people process how they're growing and what's next in their life and ministry.

One of the people attending that weekend is Maria, from the Tuesday morning Bible study. She asked permission first because she wasn't sure if the weekend was just for church people. But just as some of her friends in the Bible study had assured her, it was totally fine for her to go along.

In her study of Jesus in the gospel of Mark, Maria had gotten the idea that she should be reaching out to her neighbors and helping them more than she had been. Even if she wasn't sure about Jesus being God, that much certainly seemed like a good idea. By the end of the weekend, Maria came away with some ideas about how she could show love to her neighbors. It was almost like God was speaking to her.

• • • • •

Aaron went to the discipleship weekend too. Having just come through a bitter divorce, he felt the need to reconnect with God and repair his spiritual life. He knew he was in need of healing. After talking with one of the Barnabases, Aaron came away with a new approach to engaging with God. He began to feel just the beginning of hope that he could experience God's grace and love again.

· · · · ·

Justin came away from his time at the discipleship weekend with a new vision for service. He had known for a while that he wanted to serve as a volunteer at a halfway house, but hadn't realized until now that he didn't want to do it alone. He wanted to lead a team from the church. That was what had been holding him up. When Justin got back from the weekend, he put in a request to the elder board to approve this new ministry team.

· · · · ·

The elder board had a long history of planning… and moving forward only with those plans that had originated *from* the elder board. When the proposal to start a ministry at a halfway house came up, most people's instinct was to table it: Maybe next year, but for now we have other priorities.

But one board member asked, "What if this is something God wants to us to do? How would we know?" He suggested approving the new ministry team on a trial basis and then evaluating the ministry again after three months.

The new ministry saw a surprising amount of fruit given the low cost of investment. In this way, a new ministry emerged through which the church was able to bless the community.

· · · · ·

After reflecting on some of their recent successes, including the ministry at the halfway house, the discipleship weekend, and the Dimensions of Discipleship materials being used in one of their missional communities, the elder board decided to offer Barnabas training to the congregation. They tapped Dana, the missional community leader, to facilitate the training since she had been trained as a Barnabas earlier.

Dana now enjoys passing along her Barnabas skills to others, as well as helping people new to the congregation find a meaningful place of service that is in line with how God made them and what he is calling them toward.

· · · · ·

And remember Chad? The engineer who took a leave of absence to become a teacher for a semester? He decided to return to his engineering job, but with an added role. His company has agreed to have Chad coordinate a volunteer teaching program for employees, in which engineers teach inner city students and encourage them in the math and engineering fields.

Chad began leading a team of four volunteers at work and is learning how to be a positive spiritual influence in his workplace. This time around, Chad likes his job much better. He feels it's precisely where God wants him right now.

· · · · ·

Consider the passages below. Who might God speak to? What difference might they make?

Now Samuel did not yet know the LORD: The word of the LORD had not yet been revealed to him. A third time the LORD called, "Samuel!" And Samuel got up and went to Eli and said, "Here I am; you called me." Then Eli realized that the LORD was calling the boy. So Eli told Samuel, "Go and lie down, and if he calls you, say, 'Speak, LORD, for your servant is listening.'" So Samuel went and lay down in his place. The LORD came and stood there, calling as at the other times, "Samuel! Samuel!" Then Samuel said, "Speak, for your servant is listening." (I Samuel 3:7-10)

Now Moses was tending the flock of Jethro his father-in-law, the priest of Midian, and he led the flock to the far side of the wilderness and came to Horeb, the mountain of God. There the angel of the LORD appeared to him in flames of fire from within a bush. Moses saw that though the bush was on fire it did not burn up. So Moses thought, "I will go over and see this strange sight—why the bush does not burn up." When the LORD saw that he had gone over to look, God called to him from within the bush, "Moses! Moses!" And Moses said, "Here I am." (Exodus 3:1-4)

The virgin's name was Mary. The angel went to her and said, "Greetings, you who are highly favored! The Lord is with you." Mary was greatly troubled at his words and wondered what kind of greeting this might be. But the angel said to her, "Do not be afraid, Mary; you have found favor with God.... "I am the Lord's servant," Mary answered. "May your word to me be fulfilled." Then the angel left her. (Luke 1:27-30, 38)

Then I heard the voice of the Lord saying, "Whom shall I send? And who will go for us?" And I said, "Here am I. Send me!" (Isaiah 6:8)

Reflection questions:
1. Imagine Barnabases throughout your church. What might your ministry look like? What would be different?
2. What areas of your church might see positive change?
3. Who might be empowered as they listen to the voice of the Holy Spirit for his direction?

Chapter 5

How can you develop a Barnabas culture?

Practical steps and options

What if you not only want to become more of a Barnabas yourself, but also want to see others around you become Barnabases? Whether you're a pastor or a lay leader, this chapter lays out several different approaches for helping spread Barnabas ministry within your church.

As you look over some of the approaches described here, consider your own role. You may or may not have the authority to implement some of these approaches in a formal capacity. That's okay. Never underrate the potential of grassroots influence. Generally speaking, the best way to implement anything is to live into it and let others see the results. Having something catch on organically is much more powerful than trying to mandate change from the top down.

Another matter to consider is the size, structure, and culture of your ministry environment. An approach that works well in one context may not work at all in another. Consider what has been effective in the past and pray about how to implement Barnabas ministry. The best approach varies widely; do what is most likely to work in your context.

The most important thing is to move from *thinking* about a Barnabas culture to actually *implementing* a Barnabas culture. You may take some wrong turns on the way, but we all have to start somewhere. You'll learn as you go what strategies work best in your context. The key is to take some concrete steps. Feel free to adapt one of the approaches described here or even design your own.

Options for implementation:

I'm sure there are many more ways to implement Barnabas ministry, but here are some that I've thought of. Consider how each could look in your ministry context.

Serve as a Barnabas yourself

The very best way to get started is by beginning to serve as a Barnabas yourself. You can start with just the material in this book, or you can add some Barnabas coach training. But get started right away by serving as a Barnabas to those around you: your family, your friends, the people in your small group or service team. They'll notice the difference, you can explain what you're doing, and they can begin learning as well.

Lead as a Barnabas

Consider your role. Are you leading a volunteer worship team? Are you facilitating a small group? Are you teaching children's classes? Are you helping others engage in missional ministry?

In whatever capacity you're leading, you can improve by listening to those you lead, asking them questions, and unpacking their thinking. You can help them listen to the Holy Spirit to see where he is leading them. You can empower them to a more powerful ministry by giving them a sounding board that helps them determine their direction and next steps.

Participate in peer Barnabas relationships

You and a couple of other people can agree to serve as Barnabases to one another. For example, let's say you are leading a community group. You could gather monthly with two other community group leaders and spend 30 minutes focusing on each of you: listening, encouraging, clarifying, brainstorming, troubleshooting, praying. You'll be amazed at how fruitful such a time can be. I call these gatherings of three "triads."

Those of you who know me know of my fondness for triads. I came up with the concept while working with a group that disliked hierarchy. In some settings, a Barnabas can be misinterpreted as a supervisor or somehow "above" other people. A more accurate interpretation, of course, is as a servant.

However, in many cases, a challenge gives rise to a good solution. Triads are peer groups of three. No one is "in charge," and all three can serve as Barnabases to the others in turn. I've found that groups of four aren't able to give enough individualized attention to each member. Groups of two can become competitive if one person is perceived as doing "better" than the other. But groups of three can serve one another very effectively.

Train more Barnabases

An additional way to spread Barnabas ministry throughout your context is to develop more Barnabases. Some people like to coach individually, but don't think about the potential benefits to the larger ministry if coaching spreads. Spread it by raising up more Barnabases. We have tools you can use do that at the grassroots level. See the list of resources later in this chapter for some tools that might be helpful to you.

You can start in just your area of ministry, or you can offer Barnabas training to anyone who is interested. In either case, it's best to make any training opt-in. That way you don't have to convince people to go along with something they're not ready to try.

Once you have some trained people, you can then make them available to serve others. Those who were uncertain about it can see the effects and then decide whether to go forward with it themselves. In this way, Barnabas ministry can spread organically throughout the church.

Develop Barnabases within one ministry area

Another way to create a Barnabas culture is to start in just one ministry. If your church is more traditionally structured, you could start developing Barnabases just within the small groups ministry or just within the children's ministry. The advantage of this approach is that you're able to try out Barnabas ministry on a smaller scale to see how it works before trying to implement it system-wide.

This strategy can also be effective in churches that are more hesitant to change the way things are done. This way people can see the impact on one ministry area before deciding whether it would be helpful in their ministry areas as well. Usually when people see the positive impact of successful Barnabas ministry, they are more open to trying it. You can strategically decide what area of your church would be the best place to start.

Train a few people in each ministry area to shepherd the others

It's also possible to train a few people in each ministry area as Barnabases. They can then serve other leaders as needed. For example, you could train three of the most experienced and effective small group leaders. They would then be available to help newer group leaders think through how best to lead their groups.

This approach combines Barnabas ministry with a mentor approach. It's best here to allow people to opt in to a relationship instead of assigning everyone to a Barnabas. You also have to be sure your Barnabases can refrain from giving advice in their area of expertise, because the power of the role is in listening and asking good questions.

Pastor as Barnabas

Much of real leadership is communicated by example. What people see the pastor doing, they understand as a real value – regardless of what values are being promoted verbally. By getting some training as a Barnabas and modeling good listening and question-asking skills, pastors can demonstrate firsthand the value a Barnabas brings.

Pastors often find Barnabas skills particularly helpful, since people regularly come to them for advice. By asking people questions and helping them listen to the Holy Spirit and think through what God is calling them to do, pastors can actually be more effective. In addition to avoiding taking everything on their own shoulders, pastors are helping to mature and empower their people while still being helpful to them.

Train staff to serve as Barnabases

If you have associate pastors or multiple people on your church's staff, you can provide them all with training to serve as Barnabases. The same strategy can be used with different structures of ministry: you can train your elders to serve as Barnabases, or your small group leaders, or your missional community leaders, or your ministry team leaders... whoever your next tier of leadership is.

This approach provides the benefit of many more Barnabases throughout the organization, multiplying the impact on your ministry culture. Don't forget though that these leaders-- whether they are staff, elders, group leaders, or ministry team leaders-- will need someone to serve as a Barnabas to them. They will need support to continue to serve in this capacity over the long haul.

What works?

As you consider the implementation strategies listed above, what do you think might work well in your context? What might not work well?

Dealing with common challenges

When implementing Barnabas ministry, certain common problems may arise and we want to help you think through those issues. Some of the most common are listed below, as well as suggestions on how to approach them.

Fizzle out

One of the most common problems church leaders face is fizzle out. We start strong, we're going to do this... then the enthusiasm fades, and the Barnabas activities fade along with it. I see this same cycle with many other implementation attempts, not just Barnabas ministry. The same fizzle out cycle can be seen in social justice activities, financial giving campaigns, church health initiatives, missional engagement, evangelism efforts, the list goes on.

The dynamics behind it are the same regardless of the issue, and repeated fizzle outs can do much more damage to the church than is often realized. Essentially, when leaders continue to bring forward initiatives and then let them fizzle out, they're training their people not to take them seriously. The people think, "I guess this Barnabas thing is the next new fad. I won't do much about it because it will be gone in six months." The recipe for preventing this kind of damage is a combination of modeling, consistency, and support.

- Modeling: If the senior leaders aren't engaged in an activity – whether it's Barnabas ministry or evangelism or small groups – almost everyone else will assume it's not very important.

- Consistency: This is just old-fashioned stick-to-it-ness. If you commit to something over the long haul, it will eventually catch on.

- Support: Some sort of support structure is needed for new ministries. Sometimes it's funding or staff hours. In the case of Barnabas ministry it can often be something like disciple.mycoachlog.com, an online system that keeps Barnabas relationships on track. Or it can be monthly gatherings where everyone who serves as a Barnabas comes together for support, prayer, and encouragement.

Modeling, consistency, and support all work together to encourage longevity in any endeavor, and Barnabas ministry is no exception.

Resistance to authority

In some settings, people intuitively resist the idea of having someone else in "authority" over their ministry. A reporting structure can leave some people feeling as if they are not trusted to make their own ministry decisions.

Even a brief experience with Barnabas ministry will dispel these beliefs, particularly when the Barnabas listens and empowers rather than telling people what to do. However, if the resistance is strong, a peer structure of Barnabas ministry (I am Barnabas to you, just as you are Barnabas to me) can be helpful. See the triad approach described earlier.

Resistance to oversight by lay leaders

In some settings, people resist oversight by lay leaders. They feel they should only "report" to someone in a formal pastoral position. Part of this resistance is similar to the misinterpretation of Barnabas ministry referenced earlier – it's not a position of authority, but of service.

However, at a deeper level, this is essentially a theological issue that does not fully take into account the priesthood of all believers. All believers are called to make use of their giftedness, and there is no reason to restrict Barnabas ministry to clergy.

Here are a few possible ways to approach this challenge:

- Theological education: Plan sermons or other teaching on spiritual gifts, leadership, servanthood, and the role of clergy.

- Barnabas education: Clarify the servant role of a Barnabas through training, demonstration, and modeling.
- Renaming: Depending on your denominational tradition, those serving as Barnabases to others could be considered – and called – elders, deacons, or deaconesses.

Not viewed as helpful

The two main reasons people view Barnabas ministry as not helpful are 1) they haven't experienced it at a personal level, and 2) they haven't received good training in it.

When people aren't able to see or experience Barnabas ministry in practical ways, they don't understand its power or the impact it can have. They need to understand it not only intellectually but experientially. They need to have someone serve as a Barnabas to them.

For this reason, any Barnabas training in your church must be filled with practical exercises, examples, and demonstrations. Training should also lead directly to real life application of the concepts learned. Skills we don't practice, we lose.

Not catching on

Sometimes when a new idea or approach is introduced, it just doesn't seem to gain traction – it doesn't catch on. When this happens with Barnabas ministry in churches, the core of the problem is usually a lack of modeling by the leadership. If the pastors are modeling Barnabas behaviors, not only will people experience the benefits firsthand, but they will recognize that it's important.

People regularly look to their leaders for cues as to what is truly important and what is not. When people experience Barnabas ministry and see their leaders engaging in it, Barnabas ministry will catch on.

Resources to help you along the way

You could just go forward with this book and nothing else. The basic principles are here. However, if you'd rather not reinvent the wheel, you're welcome to make use of the some of the resources below. As you select resources, keep in mind your unique ministry context and adapt accordingly.

- **This book**. *Becoming Barnabas* is a great starting point. If you want to start spreading the word within your ministry, get some copies of this book to your key leaders.
- **Barnabas coach training**. I've teamed up with Dave DeVries to offer Barnabas coach training designed for local churches and ministries. Taken in bite-sized chunks, you can work it into your regularly scheduled leader meetings. The training is video-based, and includes practical exercises to help people get some practice. The entire training can be done at your location with someone from your group facilitating.
- **Coaching 101**. For people who want to go deeper into Barnabas ministry, *Coaching 101* gets into further details on how to serve effectively as a coach (aka Barnabas).
- **The Dimensions of Discipleship assessment and coaching guides**. If one of your main aims in developing a Barnabas ministry is discipleship, you can use the *Dimensions of Discipleship* materials in tandem with guidance from a Barnabas. An initial assessment helps people discern where they are and where they need to grow in their discipleship journey. They can then work through the corresponding guides for whichever areas are needed.

The Dimensions of Discipleship

- Experiencing God
- Spiritual responsiveness
- Sacrificial service
- Generous living
- Disciplemaking
- Personal transformation
- Authentic relationships
- Community transformation

These eight elements form the basis of both discipleship AND leadership. Discipleship is actually the missing ingredient in most leadership development programs. We can't make effective leaders out of people who are not first disciples. See www.discipleassessment.com/resources for more information on how you can implement *The Dimensions of Discipleship* in your ministry.

Conclusion

Choose an approach for developing a Barnabas culture that will work in your ministry structure. Contextualization is important because this relational approach becomes the ethos of who you are as a church and how you come alongside people.
Regardless of which method you decide to use, make sure you are consistent and intentional in implementing it. Without that intentionality, potential is wasted. With it, you'll see fruit beyond what you imagined.

When you have a system of coming alongside people and developing them over the long haul, you will see people healed, disciples developed, leaders raised, ministry enhanced, and glimpses of the Kingdom as the Holy Spirit does his work.

As a result of coaching, people not only grow in their discipleship, they increasingly live incarnationally, minister out of compassion, develop new leaders, and even raise up church planters. Coaching impacts not just the individual, but the entire community.

For a couple of years now, Madison Vineyard Church has been running an internship program in which they offer coaching to those who want to develop as leaders. They've seen people receive clarity about their calling, as well as thinking through obstacles and options in a different way than they normally would. That impact has radiated throughout their community as a result of the experiences of those leaders.

One woman who had started an intercession ministry at the church was a bit skeptical about coaching. By nature she was not very structured and was resistant to the idea of a coach driving the agenda for her prayer ministry. Yet her experience of coaching did not line up with those concerns. Instead, she took away some helpful action items from the coaching relationship – action items she herself came up with. Some of those action items were personal – ways to grow in her own prayer life. Other action items applied more broadly. One new idea she implemented moved the prayer ministry forward more than it had in the last three years.

Another man served in the small group ministry. Receiving coach training helped him become a better listener, creating space for people to process their thoughts. An extrovert by nature, he had tended to fill the space quickly whenever there was silence. Yet he learned to dial that tendency back when he was pastoring introverts. He also learned to ask questions designed to draw people out, making his group more effective at discipling those who were a part of it.

A third person involved in the internship was leading the marriage and family ministry. She taught classes, and as a result of receiving coaching decided to also begin offering coaching once a month to people who wanted help communicating more effectively with their spouse. In this way, coaching was passed throughout the congregation in a way that made a significant impact on people's everyday lives.

The pastor of Madison Vineyard put it this way: "I believe we were already postured to listen to the Holy Spirit, but coaching has taken that to a new level. It's put structure and words to how we go about listening to God and how we draw one another out as we process what we are hearing from God."

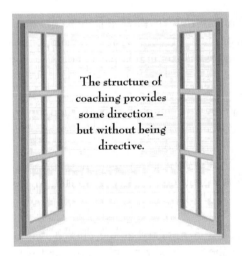

The structure of coaching provides some direction – but without being directive.

Coaching has also impacted discipleship relationships, especially for people who are newer to the faith. Asking questions in the context of community provides a safety net as they are learning to discern God's voice. Rather than trying to hear from God on their own, they can learn to do it alongside others, checking what they are hearing and learning. As a result, the new disciples are growing stronger and learning how to discern God's voice alongside others. The structure of coaching provides some direction – but without being directive.

At the church's board meeting last month, one leader modeled coaching skills by asking questions: "What's clear?" "What's not clear?" The whole approach to the meeting was so different from the traditional agenda. Discussion was fruitful, yielding much more ownership than usual; everyone left with a clear understanding of their own strategies for taking the decisions they had made to different segments of the congregation.

Madison Vineyard is now coaching another church that would like to develop a similar coaching-based internship program. It's been something beneficial to them that they can now offer to others. And so we see the yeast working through the whole batch of dough:

"The Kingdom of Heaven is like the yeast a woman used in making bread. Even though she put only a little yeast in three measures of flour, it permeated every part of the dough."(Matthew 13:33)

Where do you go from here?

1. What are the first steps you personally are going to take?
2. How can you help others get started on this journey?
3. Who might be interested in this type of ministry?
4. How will you implement Barnabas ministry in your context?
5. What kind of help or resources do you need to get started?

Called Alongside to Help

Barnabas Coach Training makes developing quality coaches at the grassroots level possible.

Barnabas Coach Training is a turnkey system that develops coaches within a local church or ministry. Any leader can facilitate this training...

- without flying your people to a training event
- without hiring a trainer to come in and speak to your people
- without asking your laypeople to commit large chunks of time

This training process is comprised of six sessions, which can be spread out over six months. Each session focuses on a different aspect of coaching, and the timing allows people to put what they are learning into practice. Some basic content is delivered via video, and then an on-site facilitator can walk people through the exercises and discussions to help them process and practice the concepts.

Barnabas Coach Training system integrates with Disciple.MyCoachLog.com to maximize impact.

Find out more and order at:
missionaltoolkit.com

Dimensions of Discipleship

Your ministry will only grow as well
as the disciples that you develop.

Go to disciple.mycoachlog.com to make disciples
who live and love like Jesus.

Making Life Count

By Robert Logan and Tara Miller

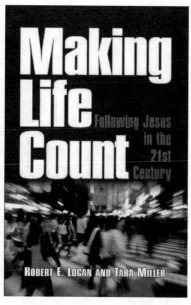

Most of the time it's the simple stuff that derails our discipleship ...

We all have dreams and desires. We want to feel like we're making a difference in this world, contributing our gifts and talents. We want to know that God is using us to build his kingdom. We may even want to be a leader someday. But we also have challenges and distractions, problems and obstacles. And we're often not sure how to get around them.

Most of the time it's the simple stuff that derails our discipleship: Low on time, low on money, losing track of what we were supposed to be doing. Our lives just don't seem in order. We're like a wagon in the mud: we want to move forward, but we just keep getting stuck. Sometimes we're just spinning our wheels; other times it feels like the wheels are going to come right off. We feel overloaded and overwhelmed.

Making Life Count is for you who want to:

- have time to do what you really want to do
- feel like you're moving in a clear direction
- stop feeling caught in the rat race
- know that your life is counting for something

The goal of *Making Life Count* is to combine basic discipleship with basic life skills to help people achieve the kind of life they want

This book and other resources by Bob Logan are Tara Miller are available from:

www.ChurchSmart.com
1-800-253-4276